# 101 HOPELESSLY HILARIOUS JOKES

by Lisa Eisenberg and Katy Hall

illustrated by Don Orehek

SCHOLASTIC INC.
New York Toronto London Auckland Sydney

ISBN 0-590-43636-8

12 11 10 9 8 7                    1 2 3 4 5/9

Printed in the U.S.A.                    01

First Scholastic printing, June 1990

*To two big jokers:*
*Eric Raicovich and Tommy Eisenberg*

# ALIENS!

Where should a 500-pound alien go?

*On a diet!*

What is an alien's normal eyesight?

*20–20–20!*

When you run into a three-headed alien, what should you say?

*Good-bye, good-bye, good-bye!*

**Bea:** Have you heard all the jokes about the aliens in the flying saucers?
**Dee:** No.
**Bea:** Never mind. They're over your head!

Why should you never insult an alien?

*It might get its feelers hurt!*

How does an alien count to 23?

*On its fingers!*

# BEWITCHED!

Why was the witch first in her class?

*She was the best speller.*

How many witches does it take to change a light bulb?

*Only one — but she changes it into a toad!*

What do you call two witches who live together?

*Broom-mates.*

How can you tell twin witches apart?

*You can't always tell which witch is which.*

What is the first thing a witch does when she checks into a hotel?

*She calls Broom Service.*

**Frankenstein:** Gee, I'm thirsty.
  Could you make me a lemonade?
**Witch:** Poof! You're a lemonade!

# CREATURE FEATURE

How does a pig get to the hospital?

*In a hambulance!*

Why are skunks so smart?

*They have a lot of scents!*

Why is it hard to carry on a
conversation with a goat?

*They're always butting in!*

# CREATURE TV FEATURES

9:00 A.M.  Mr. Lizard's World
10:00 A.M.  Movie: The Ka-ratty Kid
11:00 A.M.  Peepers Court
12:00 P.M.  Movie: Hairy and the
                Hendersons
1:00 P.M.  Squeal of Fortune
2:00 P.M.  Doctor Hoot
3:00 P.M.  Days of Our Livestock
4:00 P.M.  Father Knows Beast
5:00 P.M.  I Love Goosey
6:00 P.M.  Movie: Bonnie and Clawed
7:00 P.M.  The Wonder Ears
8:00 P.M.  Who's the Bossy?
9:00 P.M.  dirtysomething
10:00 P.M.  Mr. Beleve-deer

# DOCTOR JOKES!

**Patient:** Doctor!
**Doctor:** Yes, what is it?
**Patient:** Will this cream you gave me clear up these red spots on my body?
**Doctor:** I *never* make rash promises!

**Nurse:** How is the girl who swallowed the quarter, doctor?
**Doctor:** No change yet!

**Patient:** Doctor, what should I do
when my ear rings?
**Doctor:** Answer it!

# EEEEEEK!

What do snakes do after they have a fight?

*They hiss and make up.*

What do you call a four-foot python?

*Shorty!*

Should you ever eat a green snake?

*NO! Wait until it ripens.*

What should you do if you can't find your snake?

*Call the Missing Pythons Bureau.*

How do you stop a snake from striking?

*Pay it decent wages.*

# FOWL JOKES!

What do you call an owl with a sore throat?

*A bird that doesn't give a hoot!*

Why did the hens refuse to lay any more eggs?

*They were tired of working for chicken feed!*

What do you get if you cross a parakeet and a lawn mower?

*Shredded tweet.*

Why don't ducks tell jokes while they are flying?

*Because they would quack up!*

How do lovebirds dance?

*Chick to chick.*

What did the chicken say when she laid a square egg?

*Ouch!*

What did the wicked chicken lay?

*Deviled eggs!*

What does an eagle like to write
with?

*A bald-point pen.*

What's got wings, feathers, and
fangs?

*Count Duckula.*

# GOING TO THE BALL?

Why was Cinderella such a bad basketball player?

*Her coach was a pumpkin.*

Why was Cinderella thrown off the baseball team?

*Because she ran away from the ball!*

What did Cinderella say when the snapshots she'd taken didn't arrive?

*Someday my prints will come!*

What does Cinderella Seal wear?

*Glass flippers!*

# HARE-Y HUMOR!

What do you call a carrot that insults a rabbit?

*A fresh vegetable!*

How do you paint a rabbit?

*With hare spray!*

Where does a bunny go when its coat
needs grooming?

*To the hare dresser.*

What did the rabbits say when the farmer caught them in the garden?

*"Lettuce alone!"*

What do you call a rabbit that likes to swim with alligators?

*Dinner.*

Where do rabbits go when they get married?

*On their bunnymoon!*

# BUNNY BEST-SELLERS

*Outfoxing Foxes*
  by Ron A. Weigh
*The Bunny Cookbook*
  by Cara Stu
*The Bunny Cookbook Two*
  by Letta Seet
*Having Big Families*
  by Y. Nott
*Successful Garden Raids*
  by Luke Sharp
*My Life as a Pet Rabbit*
  by N.D. Hutch

# I HATE DOCTOR JOKES!

**Patient:** My little boy just swallowed a roll of film!

**Doctor:** Hmmmm. Let's hope nothing develops!

**Mother:** Doctor, my baby just swallowed a pen!

**Doctor:** I'll come right over!

**Mother:** But what should I do until you get here?

**Doctor:** Use a pencil!


**Sid:** The doctor told me to drink carrot juice after a hot bath.

**Sam:** Did it help?

**Sid:** I don't know. I can never finish drinking the hot bath!

# JUDGE,
# HERE COMES THE!

What do lawyers wear to court?

*Lawsuits!*

Why did the robber take a bath?

*So he could make a clean getaway!*

What did the judge give the thief who stole the calendar?

*Twelve months!*

What did the judge say when she got home from work?

*"It's been a trying day!"*

What did the thief say when he robbed the glue factory?

*This is a stickup!*

# Kangaroo korner!

What do you get if you cross a
kangaroo and an elephant?

*Giant holes all over Australia!*

What did the mother kangaroo say
when her baby was lost?

*My pocket's been picked!*

# KANGAROO PROFILE

**AGE TEN, NEXT LEAP YEAR**

**FAVORITE SONGS:**
AT THE TOP, PAL JOEY,
HOPPY BIRTHDAY

**FAVORITE SEASON:** SPRING

**FAVORITE DESSERT:**
PINEAPPLE
UPSIDEDOWNUNDER CAKE,
KANGAROOBARB PIE

**FAVORITE ACTIVITIES:** GOING TO
LEAPOVER PARTIES

**BIGGEST FAULT:** REMEMBERING TO
STAY INSIDE THE BOUNDS

**PET PEEVE:** WHEN HER BABY EATS
CRACKERS IN BED

Why do mother kangaroos hate rainy days?

*Because the children have to play inside!*

# LETTERS, WE GET LETTERS!

Dear Lisa & Katy:
  I know lots of jokes that would be great in your books! Can I send you my collection of bowling riddles?
    Signed,
    Ina Gutter

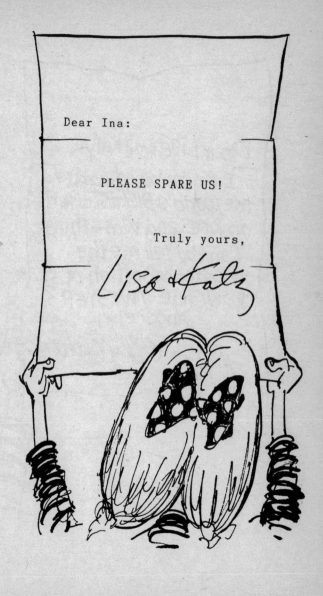

Dear Polly:

It's when your tang
gets all tongueled up!

Best wishes,

Lisa & Katy

# Monster madness!

Why was Dr. Frankenstein never lonely?

*He was good at making new friends!*

Why did the invisible man's girlfriend understand him so well?

*She could see right through him!*

Why did King Kong climb the Empire State Building?

*He wanted to catch a plane!*

What happened to the Frankenstein
monster that was built upside down?

*His feet smelled and his nose ran!*

**Answer:** *Club sandwich.*
**Question:** What did the monster do
to make his lunch hold still?

What did the Frankenstein monster
say to his bride?

*"You are so electrocute!"*

# No! no! not more DOCTOR JOKES!

**Daffynition:** A medicine dropper is a doctor with butter on his hands!

How long should a doctor practice medicine?

*Until he gets it right!*

Why did the doctor take his eye chart into the classroom?

*He wanted to check the pupils!*

**Patient:** Doctor, my little brother is really crazy! He thinks he's a chicken!

**Doctor:** How long has this been going on?

**Patient:** For six years.

**Doctor:** Good heavens! Why have you waited so long to come for help?

**Patient:** We needed the eggs!

# OPEN THE DOOR!

Knock, knock!
Who's there?
Soup!
Soup who?
Souperman!

Knock, knock!
Who's there?
Baa!
Baa who?
Baatman!

Knock, knock!
Who's there?
Cook!
Cook who?
Hey! Who are you calling cuckoo!




Knock, knock!
Who's there?
Cash!
Cash who?
Gesundheit!

Knock, knock!
Who's there?
Police!
Police who?
Police stop telling these stupid knock-
knock jokes!




Knock, knock!
Who's there?
Twig!
Twig who?
Twig or tweet!

# PLEASE! NO MORE DOCTOR JOKES!

**Cowboy:** Doctor, ever since I've been riding in the rodeo, I haven't been feeling very well. What do you think it could be?
**Doctor:** Bronc-itis!

**Kangaroo:** Doctor, I have a terrible problem.

**Doctor:** What seems to be the trouble?

**Kangaroo:** Oh, I don't know. I just haven't been feeling jumpy lately!

What did the doctor say to the tonsil?

*"You're so cute, I think I'll take you out tonight!"*

What did the doctor say to the patient when the operation was over?

*"That's enough out of you!"*

# DOCTORS TO THE STARS!

Dr. Paul Newmumps
Dr. Shirley Tempill
Dr. Lucille Bill
Dr. Joan Colics
Dr. Meryl Streepthroat
Dr. Charlton Hestonic
Dr. Tracey Illman
Dr. Pill Donahue
Dr. Candice Bergerm

# QUESTIONABLE CROSSES!

What do you get if you cross an adult with a moan?

*A groan-up!*

What do you get if you cross a bee and a telephone?

*A buzzy signal!*

What do you get if you cross a goose
with a charging bull?

*An animal that honks before it runs
you down!*

What do you get if you cross poison
ivy with a black cat?

*A rash of bad luck!*

What do you get if you cross a dentist
and a boat?

*The tooth ferry!*

What do you get if you cross a bird's
beak with a socket?

*An electric bill!*

# Ribbit riddles

Where does a frog change its clothes?

*In the croak-room!*

What happened to the frog's car when the parking meter expired?

*It got toad away!*

What do you get if you cross a frog with a soft drink?

*Croaka-Cola!*

What happened when two frogs went after the same fly?

*They became tongue-tied!*

What year do frogs like best?

*Leap year!*

What's green and jumps a foot every three seconds?

*A frog with hiccups!*

What do you get if you cross a frog and a dog?

*A croaker spaniel!*

# Skeleton sillies!

Why did one skeleton chase the other?

*He had a bone to pick with him!*

What musical instrument did the skeleton play?

*The trombone!*

How did the skeleton know it was raining?

*He could feel it in his bones.*

**Father Skeleton:** What's junior doing with that book?
**Mother Skeleton:** He's boning up for his big test!

What do skeletons say before they
begin dining?

*Bone appetit!*

# TELL ME AGAIN

What did one strawberry say to the other?

*If you'd listened to me, we wouldn't be in this jam!*

What did the dirt say to the rain?

*If you keep this up, my name will be mud!*

What did the beaver say to the tree?

*It's been nice gnawing you!*

What did the rake say to the hoe?

*Hi, hoe!*

# Underwater riddles!

What do little sharks love to eat?

*Peanut butter and jellyfish sandwiches.*

What lies at the bottom of the ocean and shivers?

*A nervous wreck.*

Where do sharks come from?

*Sharkago.*

What day of the week do fish hate most?

*Fry-day!*

Why wasn't the girl afraid of the shark?

*It was a man-eating shark.*

# FISHY FAVORITE MOVIES

The Cod Father
Gone with the Finned
Finny Lady

# FISHY TOP TUNES

Teeth for Two
Thank Heaven for Little Gills

# VAMPIRE BITES THE DUST!

What position does Dracula play on his hockey team?

*Ghoulie.*

What does Dracula wear in the evenings?

*His batrobe.*

Why did Dracula break up with his sweetie pie?

*She wasn't his (blood) type!*


What kind of car does Dracula drive?

*A bloodmobile.*

What does Dracula like to eat at baseball games?

*Fang-furters!*

Why was Dracula glad to help young vampires?

*He liked to see new blood in the business.*

What does Dracula get when he forgets to brush his teeth?

*Bat breath!*

Will Dracula ever marry?

*No, he's a confirmed bat-chelor.*

Why is Dracula's family so close?

*Because blood is thicker than water.*

# WEREWOLF WOW-ERS!

What did the werewolf write on his Christmas cards?

*"Best vicious!"*

How does the werewolf like his eggs for breakfast?

*Terri-fried!*

What does a werewolf wear at the beach?

*Moon-tan lotion!*

**Junior:** Mom, the other kids tease me and say I'm a werewolf!
**Mom:** I've never heard such nonsense! Now go comb your face and get ready for supper.

Why does the werewolf buy a
newspaper every day?

*To check on his horrorscope.*

**Pat:** Did you hear about the werewolf that ran away with the circus?
**Nat:** No, what happened?
**Pat:** They made him give it back.

**Dracula:** How was your birthday party?
**Werewolf:** It was a howling success!

# X-RAY RIDDLE!

**Patient:** Doctor, what does the X ray of my head show?
**Doctor:** Nothing!

# YACKIE-TACKIES!

A *yacky-tacky* is a riddle with two rhyming words for its answer.

For example: What is a *yacky-tacky* for a small hot dog?

A *teeny weenie!*

What is a *yack-tack* for a great pig?

A *fine swine!*

What is a *yacky-tacky* for a stupid embalmed body?

*A dummy mummy!*

What is a *yack-tack* for a shortened black-and-white mammal?

*A shrunk skunk!*

What is a *yack-tack* for an unusual grizzly?

*A rare bear!*

What is a *yacky-tacky* for a witch doctor's mistake?

*A voodoo boo-boo!*

What is a *yacky-tacky* for a gangster shellfish?

*A mobster lobster!*

# ZEBRA RIDDLES!

What is a zebra?

*A horse with venetian blinds!*

What's black and white and red all over?

*An embarrassed zebra!*

If this book goes from A to Z, what goes from Z to A?

*A zebra!*